LIVES OF IRISH ARTISTS

Mildred A. Butler

Mildred Anne Butler
1858-1941

ANNE CROOKSHANK

Mildred A. Butler

Mildred Anne Butler
1858 - 1941

ANNE CROOKSHANK

THE NATIONAL GALLERY OF IRELAND
IN ASSOCIATION WITH
TOWN HOUSE, DUBLIN

Published in 1992 by

Town House

42 Morehampton Road

Donnybrook

Dublin 4

for The National Gallery of Ireland

British Library Cataloguing in Publication Data

Crookshank, Anne O.

Mildred Anne Butler, 1858-1941. — (Lives of Irish Artists Series)

I. Title II. Series

759.2915

ISBN: 0-948524-37-5

Acknowledgements

This text is based on research done by the author and Desmond Fitzgerald,
the Knight of Glin. The letters, account books and scrapbooks which are
quoted from belong to them. The author is grateful for information received
from Eileen Black of the Ulster Museum, who owns Miss Butler's diary, and to
Messrs Christies of London who sold Mildred Anne Butler's studio in 1981.

Cover: *A Sheltered Corner c* 1910 (Ulster Museum, Belfast)

Managing editor: Treasa Coady

Series editor: Brian P Kennedy (NGI)

Text editors: Elaine Campion, Bernie Daly

Colour origination: The Kulor Centre

Design concept: Q Design

Printed in Hong Kong

CONTENTS

Anne Crookshank has published extensively on Irish artists, the principal topic of her research. She has contributed articles on James Latham and Robert Hunter to the *Irish Arts Review* and, with Desmond Fitzgerald, the Knight of Glin, published *The Painters of Ireland* in 1978. Among her other works are *Irish Art from 1600 to the Present Day* and *Irish Sculpture from 1600 to the Present Day*, both published by the Department of Foreign Affairs.

8   The late nineteenth century in Ireland saw the emergence of women as professional artists. It is a remarkable fact that there seems to have been little objection from their families to their training, no doubt because it was an occupation which could be carried out from home. Mildred Anne Butler was one of the earliest of these pioneering women.

A COUNTRY BACKGROUND

Like most of her contemporaries, Mildred Anne Butler came from a comfortable background. Her home was Kilmurry, near Thomastown, County Kilkenny, a Georgian house standing in meadows and overlooking a lake. It had an exceedingly beautiful garden which was the particular interest of her sister Isabel. The surrounding countryside was rich farmland and Mildred lived in this rural setting throughout her life, surviving her brothers and sisters and finally inheriting Kilmurry. Very few of Mildred Anne's pictures show the romantic mountainous landscape often associated with Ireland, for though she travelled in her native country she rarely went far. Tramore, the small seaside resort in County Waterford, was a favourite with her family, and on a few occasions she records visits to west Cork, Killarney and Kerry, but she hardly ever painted elsewhere in Ireland. Her travels were more to

London in the spring to look at exhibitions, and to the continent where she went regularly between 1905 and 1914. She suffered from rheumatism, and whenever she was in France she visited Aix-les-Bains to drink the waters. When she was in Germany she consulted an oculist in Wiesbaden. She sketched in both countries and several of these pictures were later turned into finished paintings. Eventually, as her rheumatism got worse, she had to give up painting altogether. Her handwriting reveals that her hands were badly crippled from around 1920. It was in 1931, however, that she first mentioned in letters that she had not been painting. After the First World War she rarely painted outside the Kilkenny area, though she still visited London and contributed regularly to exhibitions.

INFLUENCES AND TRAINING

Mildred Anne's father, Captain Henry Butler, was the grandson of the eleventh Viscount Mountgarret. He had marked artistic talent and in 1841 he published *South African Sketches: Illustrative of the Wildlife of a Hunter on the Frontier of Cape Colony*. Over the years his style developed from these charming illustrations to the extraordinary, almost frightening drawings he did later when in the West Indies. These are unnerving in their introduction of snakes and other fauna and flora of tropical rain forests. Captain Butler died in 1881, just about the time Mildred Anne began her training as an artist, and his style does not seem to have influenced his daughter. Her earliest works dating from 1878 survive in a scrapbook and it is obvious that she was then quite untrained. This scrapbook also contains a few *11* watercolours by her brother Henry Butler, which, though not nearly as competent as his sister's, are close in style, and indicate that painting was a normal part of their lives.

Though Mildred Anne was a landscape painter all her life, peopling her scenes with cows (*Pl 1*), sheep, deer, horses, and above all birds, she was a lady of her time and felt that titles were essential, however inappropriate they may seem today. One of her notebooks, which she later used to record sales, contains quotations taken from the books she was reading and which she felt made suitable titles for her pictures. In the early 1880s when she began her training, even the tiniest sketches sent to her master for comment were given splendid titles. From the beginning she used photographs as an aid: a portrait of a dog and the outside of an English church were both painted from photographs in her scrapbook.

Mildred Anne's first master was Paul Jacob Naftel,

a landscape artist who lived in London and painted in watercolour. He was renowned as a teacher. He came from the Channel Islands and exhibited twice in the Royal Hibernian Academy, in 1860 and 1862, on the latter occasion giving a Guernsey address. He may have been known to the Butler family as he visited Ireland during this time. Mildred Anne seems to have sent him a portfolio of drawings and watercolours each month, which he would mark and return, sometimes adding his comments. Most of those which have survived are on separate sheets of notepaper and unfortunately they do not relate to extant drawings but they are full of very constructive criticism. Clearly Naftel felt that she was very good and was concerned that she lacked confidence. In an undated note he wrote '...the marvellous change in your work and perception in something less than three years I should think had never been seen before. I really cannot find fault with them [the drawings] and you must go on working in the same spirit with full confidence — no more doubt as to whether you can or this or that — do it, and don't have the least doubt but that you can do it better than any one else...'. In the only dated letter, of 20 February 1885, he says 'The little help I have had the pleasure of offering you has been of an irregular character'. In fact Naftel was a major influence on her career and her early exhibited drawings show some of the meticulous detail which

cont. p25

12

ILLUSTRATIONS

PLATE 1

A Sheltered Corner *c* 1910

13

Pl 1   From the coarse winter grass and the group of cows in the foreground to the long shadowed fields stretching far back into the picture plane, and the rain-laden sky, this splendid picture epitomises Mildred Anne Butler's perception of nature.

Watercolour on paper; signed; 52.5 x 71.2 cm
Ulster Museum, Belfast

PLATE 2

Girl with a Basket Walking Through an Orchard

Pl 2   T*his is one of the pictures which suggests that Mildred Anne Butler knew the work of the impressionists. The beautifully handled foreground meadow contrasts with the blue shadows of the trees.*

Watercolour heightened with white on paper; 27.3 x 37.1 cm
Private collection
(Photo courtesy of Christies, London)

14

Mildred A. Butler

PLATE 3

The River Nore at Thomastown

15

Pl 3   **M**ildred Anne Butler was expert in her handling of washes. In this sensitive watercolour she so beautifully conveys a gentle evening light.

Watercolour on paper; 18.4 x 26 cm
Private collection

Pl 4   T*his is a typical example of Mildred Anne Butler's large exhibition watercolours. It was exhibited at the Royal Academy in 1899. Despite its rather grand title, it shows the pigeons at her home finding an open sack of grain.*

16

Watercolour on paper; 65.6 x 97.5 cm
National Gallery of Ireland

Pl 5   K*ilmurry, Mildred Anne Butler's home, receives lyrical handling in this watercolour. It is seen here in springtime, surrounded by newly opened trees, all reflected magically in the lake.*

Watercolour with touches of white heightening on paper; 36.8 x 53.9 cm
Private collection

PLATE 4

A Preliminary Investigation 1898

PLATE 5

Kilmurry

PLATE 6

The Lilac Phlox, Kilmurry, County Kilkenny

18

Pl 6   The Lilac Phlox *is a view of Mildred Anne Butler's favourite border in the garden at Kilmurry and was first exhibited in 1912. From the 1890s she exhibited views of the gardens of the house, which show her interest in botany. She nearly always specified the dominant flowers in the titles of her paintings.*

20

Watercolour on paper; signed; 36.1 x 54 cm
National Gallery of Ireland

Pl 7   This *is a lovingly portrayed view of a room in Mildred Anne Butler's home. The title,* Ancient Rubbish, *no doubt refers to the wicker basket full of waste paper in the foreground and to the general loose assortment of objects around the room.*

Watercolour on paper; 36.5 x 26.4 cm
National Gallery of Ireland

PLATE 7

Ancient Rubbish, Kilmurry

21

Pl 8   T*his rare example of a 'wild' landscape was probably painted during a holiday in the south-west of Ireland; it is a direct contrast to the lush fields of County Kilkenny. With its rather tight brushwork and luminous light, it shows the influence of Mildred Anne's first master, Paul Naftel.*

22

Watercolour on paper; 36.8 x 54.6 cm
Private collection

Pl 9   M*ildred Anne Butler painted a number of pictures of peacocks, all of which were greatly admired.* Where the Grass Grows Green *was first exhibited in 1906. The peacocks, with jewelled beauty, rise out of the lush Kilkenny grass and create a sumptuous effect.*

Watercolour on paper; signed; 50.1 x 67.3 cm
Private collection

PLATE 8

A Rocky Stream 1887

23

PLATE 9

Where the Grass Grows Green 1904

PLATE 10

A Steam Train

24

Pl 10

A Steam Train *can be dated from a sketch which is inscribed 'Tramore, July 22nd 1889'. Among Mildred Anne Butler's many family papers, there is a photograph of this train from which she clearly worked, especially in the drawing of the engine.*

Watercolour heightened with white on paper; signed;
52.7 x 36.1 cm
Private collection

cont. from p12

characterises his own work.

Mildred Anne's diaries indicate that she led a full social life in her youth and that she travelled to the continent for the first time in 1885, going via France and Switzerland to Italy with a relation, Lady French. As early as 1882 and 1883 she had shown work with an amateur society called the Irish Fine Arts Society, which had been holding exhibitions since 1871 in the provinces, and from 1877 annually in Dublin. This *25* society, which changed its name to the Watercolour Society of Ireland in 1887–8, was to have an important place in Mildred Anne's life: she not only exhibited there but was on the committee for many years. After 1883 she did not show with them again until 1889, but she exhibited there regularly from 1892. In 1888 she faced a more exacting audience as she ventured to London and showed at the Dudley Gallery, which held prestigious exhibitions. She continued with them, becoming one of their regular artists, elected to their society on the strength of her first exhibited work. Mildred Anne was to exhibit all her life, keeping careful account of the pictures she sent to each exhibition and the pictures she sold. Later, when she was making quite a lot of money, she was careful to keep her tax and financial affairs in order. In fact most of the 'lady' artists of the time seem to have been highly efficient and professional about their work. In 1896 one of Mildred Anne's watercolours was bought for the very large sum of £50, to become part of the Chantrey Bequest for the Tate Gallery.

After leaving Naftel, Mildred Anne continued her education. She spent one term at Frank William Calderon's school in London, which he founded in 1894 to teach animal painting. From there she went to Newlyn in Cornwall, studying under the Clare-born artist Norman Garstin. Garstin had lived in Tipperary, not that far from Kilmurry, before moving to Cornwall. There are letters from Stanhope Forbes and Luke Fildes discussing suitable lodgings in Newlyn, where Mildred Anne spent six weeks with May Guinness in 1894 and almost two months alone in the summer of 1895. Despite her visit abroad in 1885 Mildred Anne had never come into contact with modern French art until she went to Newlyn. Garstin knew Degas and had written about Manet. It was at this time that she began to paint from unusual viewpoints, from roof tops, down slopes and so forth, and developed her broad washes, strong colour, and understanding of sunlight and shadows. From the start she had worked directly from nature, but now she was learning more about selection.

TECHNIQUES AND SUBJECTS

Painting animals and birds from life is always a problem, and clearly it gave Mildred Anne a lot of trouble. Letters survive from 1888 and 1900 from a Mr G Pickhardt, a London taxidermist, from whom she bought stuffed specimens of ordinary birds, including ducks, woodpigeons, waterhens and rooks, presumably to study their plumage and features, as observations during flight would have been impossible. Cattle were also difficult to study, and an amusing photograph shows her painting two cows tethered in a very small enclosure (*frontispiece*). Her friends must have been alerted to her needs as one Lucy Guinness wrote from near Newcastle-on-Tyne that she had found a perfect group of crows' nests beside the railway near Chester Le Street. She invited Mildred to come and study these, but added that 'it would be rather jumpy with the trains tearing by every few minutes'. Mildred Anne's large watercolours of birds undoubtedly depended for their accuracy on stuffed examples and photographs. Yet none of this takes from the spontaneity of her work, which is one of its great qualities.

Despite the literary titles, Mildred Anne's work shows little of the sentimentality one finds in many paintings of the late nineteenth century. People do not figure largely in her paintings, and on the few

27

occasions when they form the main subject they are treated with simple directness and not picturesquely. A typical example is *Girl with a Basket Walking Through an Orchard (Pl 2)*. This thoughtful figure, going about her work, forms the centre of a landscape full of sparkling spring sunshine. The charming 'peasants round the cottage door' scenes which dominate many English watercolours from Birkett Foster onwards and which were favoured by such artists as Helen Allingham, were never imitated by Mildred Anne. She painted Thomastown (*Pl 3*) as an essay in light and colour, beautifully seen through a slight mist, but she did not go down the street and paint its inhabitants. Some of her paintings show children picking flowers for example, but they are few and far between.

Mildred Anne's finished watercolours were the result of a long and studied process. She would most likely have started off with a sketchbook full of small, slight sketches, and those chosen as likely subjects would then have been worked on, resulting in a whole series of tiny drawings. At this stage she probably drew the subject on to thin transparent paper, then traced it very lightly on to the paper or board on which she finally painted. She sometimes made full-scale studies in colour. Very little pencil shows through in her finished watercolours which are invariably fresh and quite unstudied in effect. The transparent paper stage was obviously necessary to achieve this result.

Her style after about 1895 does not change very much. There are fewer set pieces like the National Gallery of Ireland's *And Straight Against that Great Array Went Forth the Valiant Three,* dated 1893. Depicting as it does three crows sitting on a bush, apparently watching two boys in the distance flying a kite, the title does seem a little out of place, and indeed it is described by a critic in an unnamed newspaper cutting of 1893 as 'a very quaint conception, the artist having here parodied the lines from Macaulay's "Lays of Ancient Rome" '. A black and white illustration of it is printed in the article and this might be by Mildred herself, as a number of ink drawings of her paintings exist, including two of this subject. The magazine *Bazaar* gave a stern review of the same painting on 15 May 1893. They commented, 'The birds are certainly not rooks, and not quite like jackdaws, nor could any species of bird fly with such ill-matched wings.' While most critics did in fact praise the birds, Mildred Anne must have been very downcast by such negative reviews. *A Preliminary Investigation,* dated 1898 (*Pl 4*), is another work in the same vein. Her last painting of studied nature, entitled *Famine,* showed crows fighting over a piece of food in the snow. She priced it at £94, a sum which indicates how highly she regarded it. It was

29

exhibited as late as 1922. Perhaps because her hands were so seriously affected by rheumatism by then, she never attempted such detailed work again.

After the Chantrey purchase of *The Morning Bath* in 1896, the press was rarely harsh in its criticisms of her. That same year her biography and portrait appeared in endless articles, even in America. An article in the American periodical *Hearth and Home* on 15 April 1897 described how she worked out of doors and stressed that it was this method which 'gives...an actuality and a freshness that can be acquired in no other way. Miss Butler's landscape bears always the impress of truth, and the reality of her trees and fields, and, above all, her foregrounds, can scarcely escape the notice of the most casual observer'. This was very true. A particularly good example is the view of Kilmurry (*Pl 5*) seen from the far side of the lake. With its exquisite reflections and the opening leaves on the trees, it is a marvellous evocation of spring and of the inspiration which her home must have given to her. From the 1890s Mildred Anne exhibited views of the gardens of the house which show her interest in botany. She nearly always specified the dominant flowers in the titles of her paintings. Her love for a particular path which was bordered by flower beds and backed by trees, and which ended in a gate in the wall, is evident. This spot is painted from every aspect and in each season:

her sister sits on a chair reading in it, the tabby cats chase birds along it, and one begins to know it with its different planting from summer to summer. Many full-size study drawings survive in which the highlights are left suggested by the white paper and the flowers are not sufficiently detailed to recognise, though such lovely fresh work is as attractive today as the finished watercolour. The example in the National Gallery of Ireland, *The Lilac Phlox (Pl 6)*, *31* was first exhibited in 1912. Sometimes Mildred Anne combines two of her main interests, gardens and birds. Birds, which had in her youth been her *chefs d'oeuvre*, form the shadowy centre of her superbly romantic watercolour of wistaria and roses climbing up around an open window in *Kilmurry, An Upper Window*. A girl can be seen dimly inside, feeding the doves on the window ledge.

At the beginning of her career Mildred Anne's work was often brownish in tone and this was noticed by the critics. We can see it today in the interiors of Kilmurry, as in *Ancient Rubbish, Kilmurry (Pl 7)*. This is an excellent example and probably dates from the late 1880s, before she would have been aware of the colours being introduced into the work of modern artists. Interiors are very rare in her work, as are dull days. She loved the spring and summer, and the clearness of a frosty morning. It is true that she painted half lights, evenings and early mornings, but she was essentially a painter of the open air — unlike her contemporary Rose Barton whose work is veiled by the atmosphere of foggy towns. She rarely attempted to paint towns, except when she was in France or Germany. Her paintings of Thomastown (*Pl 3*) and Tramore are distant views only, though she exhibited *Station cars* (jaunting cars outside a Dublin station) in Dublin in 1899. There are a few landscapes with this brown tonality, for example such early works as the view of a mountain stream dated 1887 (*Pl 8*), which may well recall a Kerry holiday. *Bazaar*, with its jaundiced eye, eventually noticed it on 6 June 1898 when they remarked that this landscape was 'one of those brown-toned, somewhat sunless landscapes Miss M A Butler affects'. A year earlier on 5 May 1897 the *Atheneum* had made a more fair judgement of her current and future work. Their critic wrote '...she can make good pictures out of simple and, indeed, trivial materials...there is not a shred of a story, anecdote, incident, or an atom of pathos beyond that which always attends really artistic representations of homely nature.... These pictures command attention by the massing and breadth of their chiaroscuro, and the solid way in which they have been handled'.

One of Mildred Anne's few exotic subjects was peacocks. These were very popular and she exhibited them on and off throughout her career. She even gave one to Rose Barton in exchange for one of her drawings. *Where the Grass Grows Green* (*Pl 9*) was exhibited in 1906. It has all the jewelled beauty of a peacock surrounded by the lush grass of high summer. Amusingly, when she was sending work to an exhibition in Japan, Reginald Hunt of the Royal Watercolour Society wrote on 31 May 1921 asking her not to send peacocks as the Japanese would prefer her 'beautiful crows & meadows & sheep *33* scenes'. Occasionally Mildred Anne painted industrial machinery, like a steam engine at work threshing, or even a railway train. The latter, seen puffing its way out of the sheds at Tramore (*Pl 10*), was based on a photograph, though she must also have seen the hissing engines as she captures the steam very accurately.

❧

INTERNATIONAL RECOGNITION

Not surprisingly Mildred Anne's pictures sold well. As early as 1893 she contributed to a portfolio of drawings given by the Society of Lady Artists to Princess May (later Queen Mary) on her marriage to the Duke of York. Queen Alexandra bought one of her watercolours in 1910, though she had already been given one in 1896. Mildred Anne was asked to give a drawing to a portfolio which was presented to Queen Mary's daughter, Princess Mary (later Princess Royal), on her marriage in 1922, and in 1924 she painted a tiny watercolour of rooks (1.5 x 1 inch) for Queen Mary's doll's house. 'Society' loved her pictures, but many of the purchasers seem to have been quite ordinary people both in London and Dublin. Her work was also bought by museums from Belfast to Huddersfield. She was asked to exhibit in Hesse-Darmstadt in 1911, where the Grand Duke bought two paintings, in Japan in 1921 and in numerous shows apart from the normal round. She was invited to join the Union Internationale des Beaux-Arts et des Lettres in 1914, and flattering criticisms of her work appeared in French magazines, which would suggest that she must have exhibited there also. The largest sum she recorded making was in 1920, £209 18s 0d, and she recorded her expenses as about £30. This was exceptional as she was often paid less that £50, and it was fortunate for her that she was not financially dependent on her work. Mildred Anne was fussy about hanging and framing and in 1907 she drew out a wall to show how she wanted her work hung in an exhibition. She became an Associate of the Royal Society of Watercolour Painters in 1896 but was not made a full member until 1937, by which time she was no longer able to paint.

Mildred Anne Butler fills us with nostalgia for a lost world, the apparently endless, happy summers of Edwardian times. She avoids all social comment, misses out on political upheavals and even the Great War. Her paintings reflect none of the pain or sadness she must have suffered. She remained a quiet country gentlewoman throughout her life. The early newspapers' 'society' columns mention that she was smartly dressed and her engraved portrait shows that she was pretty. But we have no idea what her views were or what interests she had outside of her art. Perhaps it is best that she has left us to people her world, to dream of sunlight and animals, birds and flowers, of peace, happiness and prosperity. It is enough, and we should not ask for more.